The
Reading/Writing
Teacher's
Companion

EXPERIMENT
WITH
FICTION

The Reading/Writing Teacher's Companion

The
Reading/Writing
Teacher's
Companion

EXPERIMENT WITH FICTION

Donald H. Graves

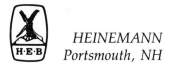

HEINEMANN
Portsmouth, NH

IRWIN PUBLISHING
Toronto, Canada

HEINEMANN EDUCATIONAL BOOKS, INC.
361 Hanover Street
Portsmouth, NH 03801
Offices and agents throughout the world

Published simultaneously in Canada by
Irwin Publishing

1800 Steeles Avenue West   Concord, Ontario, Canada L4K 2P3

The author and publisher wish to thank the following for permission to reprint previously published material:

Pages 8–9, 27, 28: From John Gardner, *The Art of Fiction: Notes on Craft for Young Writers* (New York: Vintage Books, 1985). Reprinted by permission of Alfred A. Knopf, Inc.

Pages 10–11: From Ellen Blackburn Karelitz, "Stories Never End," in *Breaking Ground: Teachers Relate Reading and Writing in the Elementary School,* ed. Jane Hansen, Thomas Newkirk, and Donald Graves (Portsmouth, NH: Heinemann, 1985). Reprinted by permission of the author.

Pages 17, 21, 32: Excerpts from *A Wrinkle in Time* by Madeleine L'Engle. Copyright © 1962 by Madeleine L'Engle Franklin. Reprinted by permission of Farrar, Straus and Giroux, Inc.

Pages 18, 19, 33: From *Katie Morag and the Two Grandmothers* by Mairi Hedderwick. Copyright © 1985 by Mairi Hedderwick. Reprinted by permission of Little, Brown and Company.

Every effort has been made to contact the copyright holders and the children and their parents for permission to reprint borrowed material. We regret any oversights that may have occurred and would be happy to rectify them in future printings of this work.

Library of Congress Cataloging-in-Publication Data

Graves, Donald H.
  Experiment with fiction.

  (The Reading/writing teacher's companion)
  Bibliography: p.
  Includes index.
  1. Creative writing (Elementary education)
2. Fiction—Study and teaching (Elementary)
I. Title. II. Series.
LB1576.G7274 1989   372.6'23   88-26835
ISBN 0-435-08485-2

Canadian Cataloguing in Publication Data

Graves, Donald H.
  Experiment with fiction.

(The Reading/writing teacher's companion)
ISBN 0-7725-1715-0

1. Fiction—Technique—Study and teaching
(Elementary). 2. English language—
Composition and exercises—Study and teaching
(Elementary). 3. Language arts (Elementary).
I. Title. II. Series: Graves, Donald H. The
reading/writing teacher's companion.

LB1576.G73 1989   372.6'23   C89-093197-6

Designed by Wladislaw Finne.
Printed in the United States of America.
10 9 8 7 6 5 4 3 2

To
Marion and Wilfred
Graves

Who listened to my stories
and helped me to create
still better ones.

contents

about this series

Reading and writing are both composing processes. History shows they have been kept apart. This series, The Reading/Writing Teacher's Companion, brings them together. With these books as a guide, you can explore the richness of reading and writing for yourself and for children. You can improve your own listening, experiment with learning, and recognize children's potential in reading and writing. Five books will make up the series:

- *Investigate Nonfiction.*
- *Experiment with Fiction.*
- *Discover Your Own Literacy.*
- *Build a Literate Classroom.*
- *Explore Poetry.*

The approach to teaching and learning is basically the same in all five books, although each stands alone in its focus. All five emphasize a learning style that immediately engages you in trying literacy for yourself, then the children. So much of learning is, and ought to be, experimental. A series of "Actions," experiments for personal growth and discovery in the classroom, are highlighted in the text to help you develop the kind of literate classroom you want. The Actions are ordered in such a way that you will gradually become aware of children's growing independence in some aspect of literacy. In all five books I'll be trying the experiments right along with you.

The five books stress learning within a literate community. Reading and writing are social acts in which children and teachers together share the books and authors they enjoy and their own composing in the various genres. Make no mistake, individuals are important, but good classrooms have always stressed group as well as individual responsibility.

The books also stress the importance of your own learning within a community. When you try the Actions and enter into new experiments with your teaching, you ought to consider reading and learning with colleagues in order to maximize your own efforts to grow as a professional.

acknowl-
edgments

Many persons have walked with me through this text. Some contributed their broad and rich understanding of children's literature, others were good readers of a text, and some were both.

My colleague, Jane Hansen, well-versed in children's literature and a good critic of text, has given constant encouragement throughout the writing of this volume. We have both seen our views about the relationship between reading and writing change since we first began our research in this area in Ellen Blackburn Karelitz's classroom in 1981. Many of those changing views are represented here in this text.

I have relied heavily on Nancie Atwell's knowledge and understanding of this field. Her response is specific, challenging, and encouraging. A good portion of the text in this volume has been literally read to her over the telephone. Somehow the sound of the text helps me to write when she is the listener.

Mary Ellen Giacobbe responded to the text and had good advice on the latest in children's books. Her knowledge of children and the books that will open new worlds is both thoughtful and perceptive.

Don Murray's extensive collection of professional writers' comments about the writing of fiction, and his firsthand knowledge of the craft itself, have led me to take risks I might not normally take. Our weekly luncheons served to lift me up on the difficult writing days.

The teachers at the Stratham Memorial School in Stratham, New Hampshire, showed me what was possible in the teaching of fiction through reading and writing. The 1987–88 school year saw an explosion of reading and writing fiction. Children demonstrated unusual learning because of the teachers' challenge and the opportunities they were given to read and write. They contributed much to the research in Chapter 6 of this book.

Others helped. Julie Powell and Linda Henke in the West Des Moines schools were readers and helpful respondents. Many of the students in my class in the Advanced Reading and Writing Institute of the University of New Hampshire 1988 summer session also had helpful comments.

Philippa Stratton, Editor-in-Chief at Heinemann Educational Books, has guided me through seven years of writing books. As always, her quiet questions have led to many twists and turns in writing this text. She understands theory, what helps teachers in classrooms, and how to help writers make sense.

I am grateful to Donna Bouvier, Manager of Editing and Production at Heinemann, who has given close attention to the details of moving a text from rough cut to refinement and to something readers will find pleasing to read. The personable way in which she has dealt with nagging details has made the final push for completion a pleasure.

Finally, my wife, Betty, has patiently listened through the many drafts preceding this final copy. She has that unusual knack of sensing what will be confusing to others.

experiment with fiction

I was about six years old when I composed my first piece of fiction. I didn't write it, I told it—a whopper that stirred my parents to action. Each day, when we rode past some men working on the highway I admired them because they looked strong. In the summer heat they were stripped to the waist, and their muscles rippled and glistened with the sweat of their labor. "Who are those men?" I asked my father.

"Oh, they are working for the WPA," he replied. I didn't know that WPA stood for Works Progress Administration, a program designed by President Roosevelt during the Depression to give unemployed people an opportunity to work and earn some money. I was more impressed by the power demonstrated in those working muscles. A short time later I went to the local gasoline station and candy store to buy some penny candy. Mrs. Bradley, the proprietor, enjoyed talking with children. She probably asked for any news at home, and I replied, "My Dad is going to work for the WPA." I liked the sound of the initials and the image of my father, a school principal, stripped to the waist and slamming a pick into the macadam, demonstrating the pure power of his arms.

I guess Mrs. Bradley spoke to my father about it, because Dad pulled me aside shortly after to inform me that telling stories like that wasn't to be done. But I didn't get the point. I thought the story a beautiful one, one that fit my fancy, and shortly after I told another about how Dad and I were going on a three-day overnight boat trip. That was more plausible than the first but pure fiction nonetheless. Again, Dad spoke to me. I was embarrassed, but I still didn't understand. I was so impressed by the powerful forces of the adult world and so moved by my own wishes for travel and adventure that I created stories to fill the void.

When I was five years old and in kindergarten, I used to walk down our street to the Palisades in Weehawken, New Jersey, overlooking the Hudson River, to watch the great ocean liners in the harbor. The wish to sail away on one of those ships or to command one of them was so great that one day in afternoon kindergarten at the Webster School, I looked out the window and saw the top ship of the French line, the *Normandy*, sailing down Berganline Avenue, the street adjacent to the school. Best of all, I was at the helm, and Delores Gallo, the most beautiful girl in the class, was at the curb watching me command that great ship. I remember poor Mrs. Locke, the teacher, trying to rouse me from my reverie, her voice growing louder, while my brain beat off the sound to maintain the fiction. When she finally succeeded, I remember my embarrassment on viewing her face and the cluster of grinning children's faces that surrounded her.

It was a long time before I actually wrote fiction. In my day composing in school was limited to teacher assignments on the blackboard. But I did compose fiction in play—driving trucks, fighting battles with my soldiers and ships, flying planes, discovering new lands, and hunting animals in jungles. When my mother read books to us at home I wanted to live the story. I asked my grandfather to build my brother and me a tree house in the biggest tree in the barnyard because our most recent story told about how Ned and Dick had helped their grandfather build a tree house.

I read far more fiction than I wrote. I viewed my life as boring and contained, but fiction let me travel, fight in the American Revolution, live on deserted islands, catch big fish, and begin to take part in the lives of others. I could sit in the place of a mother or father, or even girls, though I often skipped those parts in my early years. As a boy, size and power were important to me, as were travel and territory. War was fascinating, especially the growing conflict in Europe and the power of Nazi Germany.

FIRST FICTION WRITING
Children's early fiction can be bothersome. The most common teacher complaints are that children's writing is filled with violence, lacks coherence, contains a thin line of plausibility, and

has characters with little dimensionality. As one teacher put it, "When my children write, it seems that anything goes. Fiction means you can write any old way." In some sectors of the profession, teachers either outlaw fiction or say, "No fiction this year until after Christmas. Meanwhile, just write personal narrative." The examples of writing in *Writing: Teachers and Children at Work* (1983) suggested that there is little place for fiction in a writing program. That was a weakness in the book, and one I will attempt to deal with here.

Fiction should be given attention when it appears in children's writing. It can have an important place in the lives of children, but only with the teacher's help can it become an effective instrument of expression.

USING THIS BOOK   This book is designed to help you experiment with various approaches to fiction. The problem with any book, including this one, is that I can't anticipate the best starting point for each teacher. I will therefore provide a series of Actions that will encourage you to try things with your children. As their name suggests, Actions are teaching approaches that put us "in motion" with experiments in learning. Most of them also give us the opportunity to read and write fiction for ourselves. (Why should children have all the fun?) Not only will you enjoy writing fiction, but you will also begin to understand the nature of children's growth as fiction writers from the inside.

Where possible, try the Actions with a colleague so that you can share your writing and the books you read while you discuss the progress in your classrooms. You may not wish to try the same Actions together, but you will be able to share your victories and discuss some of the problems you've encountered.

Depending on how you view your learning style, you can choose one of two ways to use this book. Both are equally important. If you feel that your style of learning requires direct involvement with the children or that you work best by developing theories during practice, you may want to plunge in and work directly with children's fiction through your own writing and teaching. After trying the Actions through teaching, you can look at the background and development of children's use of fiction.

If you want to understand children's current use of fiction as a prelude to trying the teaching Actions, you can start with the second way, which involves a thorough look at the fiction in your children's folders. Remember, this is your book. You know your learning style best. Here is your chance to experiment, observe, and learn.

Approach 1:
Practice fiction with
the children

After a brief look at children's fiction, you will experiment with writing some fiction of your own. You won't be writing short stories or novels, but you will have a chance to "mess around" with some short, ten-minute experiments. These are for you. In addition to your own writing, you will take a look at how writers of children's fiction compose leads, introduce characters, use dialogue, and end their stories. You will alternate reading and writing, enjoying each through your own experiments.

As part of your own learning, you will also try some things with the children. You will find that as you compose fiction with the children you will read the fiction of other writers differently. An essential aspect of this approach involves reading aloud to the children and inviting professional authors into your classroom to discuss their work. Your conferences will change because both you and the children are experimenting with the reading and writing of fiction together. As you become more closely involved in conferences, you will wonder more about the changes you see in your own young writers. As you work with the children in the writing workshop and in conferences, and compose together as a class, you will be developing theories about children's growth in writing fiction.

Approach 2:
Examine how children
compose fiction

While you watch children compose fiction in your own classroom, I will share data from a study I have just finished on how children from grade one through grade six develop characters in their fiction. This is one of the most effective ways of examining the growth of any writer of fiction. You will see how your children create characters, describe them, have them think, and compose dialogue. There will be exceptions to the data I present, and you will generate your own theories about why children read and write fiction as they do. Just how children compose fiction is new territory.

The world of fiction is an exciting place to visit. We do it often, whether we are children or adults—from our rising in the morning until we retire at night. We make sense out of our own living fictions by reading and writing fiction ourselves. In this way we experience life several times over—for both enjoyment and learning.

fiction is for us—first

In one sense, everything we tell is a fiction. It is our version of what we think is true. If three people witness an automobile accident, they give police three accounts, often remarkably different. Although all are biased, the people weren't lying; they simply told what they thought they saw from where they stood.

Much of what I write in the personal narrative format is fiction. When I use "I," readers believe they are seeing what actually happened through my eyes. But my memory is selective; it has no choice. It tells what it remembers or wishes had happened. When I tell about my childhood, it is an adult's memory of a child's perceptions and feelings. Nevertheless, the images I compose make it possible for you to construct your own fictions and remembrances of childhood.

When I write fiction intentionally, I also choose what pleases me and what I wish to include. As the story proceeds I have less and less control over what happens. Each word is determined by what has occurred before; each word also contains my promise for future delivery. Here is the first line in a short story I am writing:

The first time Carolyn Slater made an appointment for counseling, John Robbins wasn't surprised.

I make a promise to the reader that Carolyn Slater will have at least two appointments with John Robbins—the first, no surprise, the second, a surprise.

The fiction I write is selective and carefully arranged, with promises tightly kept. Since a one-to-one account of a personal experience would bore the reader, even in personal narrative, I select to help the reader, but not with as much intention as the reader may think. To a large degree my text is predestined from the opening word and becomes more predetermined as the text expands. In my story, Carolyn Slater walked out of her first counseling session with John Robbins, but I didn't know that was going to happen until I had described Carolyn and

7

saw how John reacted to her first statements. She simply had to leave.

In *The Art of Fiction* (1985), John Gardner writes about the demands placed on a writer of fiction. Although the discipline is severe, the writer follows no set rules. Listen to Gardner's comments:

Art depends heavily on feeling, intuition and taste. It is feeling, not some rule, that tells the abstract painter to put his yellow here and there, not there, and may later tell him that it should have been brown or purple or pea-green. It's feeling that makes the composer break surprisingly from his key, feeling that gives the writer the rhythms of his sentences, the pattern of rise and fall in his episodes, the proportions of alternating elements, so that dialogue goes on only so long before a shift to description or narrative summary or some physical action. The great writer has an instinct for these things. He has, like a great comedian, an infallible sense of timing. And his instinct touches every thread of his fabric, even the murkiest fringes of symbolic structure. He knows when and where to think up and spring surprises, those startling leaps of the imagination that characterize all of the very greatest writing.

Obviously this is not to imply that cool intellect is useless to the writer. What Fancy sends, the writer must order by Judgment. He must think out completely, as coolly as any crtiic, what his fiction means, or is trying to mean. He must complete his equations, think out the subtlest implications of what he's said, get at the truth not just of his characters and action but also of his fiction's form, remembering that neatness can be carried too far, so that the work begins to seem fussy and overwrought, anal compulsive, unspontaneous, and remembering that, on the other hand, mess is no adequate alternative. He must think as cleanly as a mathematician, but he must also know by intuition when to sacrifice precision for some higher good, how to simplify, take short cuts, keep the foreground up there in the front and the background back. (p. 7)

Yet all writers, given adequate technique—technique that communicates—can stir our interest in their special subject matter, since at heart all fiction treats, directly or indirectly, the same thing: our love for people and the world, our aspirations and fears. The particular characters, actions, and settings are merely instances, variations on the universal theme. (p. 42)

OUR FICTION   Fiction comes from the same source as all writing, whether it is poetry, personal narrative, the essay, or letters. It comes from what we see and what we know. Fiction is the itch to tell a story—an unfinished story that often begins with a chance remark, a confused observation, a sense of wonderment.

We are surrounded by stories; most of them remain unfinished. I remember driving along Mill Pond Road in our town and noticing out of the window on the driver's side an elderly woman walking her dog. She was dressed in sweat togs and Adidas shoes. Usually dogs rush forward in front of their masters, but in this instance, the woman walked so quickly the dog was choking on his lead behind her. Later I wrote a short, ten-minute piece of fiction. Here is that rough draft:

Clad in polo shirt, trousers and Addidas shoes, the woman strode briskly down the path by Mill Pond Road, the lead taught behind her as a woebegone Dachshund tried to keep up with his master's fitness program.

Each day after breakfast Mrs. Tilden popped downstairs, and though 68 years old next January, swilled her orange juice, glided quickly to the front closet, grabbed her lead, snapped it on the dog attempting to lie undiscovered behind the sideboard in the dining room. "Come on, Hugo, up you go, time for our morning walk."

Hugo lifted bloodshot eyes heavenward, rolled them again in the direction of Mrs. Tilden, and dutifully lifted hind quarters, then front quarters into position.

Ellen Blackburn Karelitz, a first-grade teacher in Somersworth, New Hampshire, was bothered by how little space she and the children had in their classroom, so she sat down and wrote an imaginative piece about what might happen if they had more space (Hansen, Newkirk, and Graves 1985). Here are Ellen's words and her comments (in roman) about how she used her story to help her children:

THE GIANT CLASSROOM

The teacher came home from school. She was in a bad mood. All day the children in her small classroom struggled to find places to work. Robert and Eric were trying to build in the library area, but Jessica and Darcy were playing Concentration in the same space. The teacher was having writing conferences. Every five minutes someone yelled, "Stop it!" "I'm telling!" "You're wrecking my house!" "Hey, you're sitting on my cards!"

In the Math Area Yudy wrote on Jaime's paper, Jaime wrote on Yudy's paper. They both started to argue. There wasn't room on the table for both papers. . . .

"Why can't I have a giant classroom?" the teacher thought. "A giant classroom." Her eyes closed. She was so tired. All of a sudden the walls began to move until it seemed they became the world all around. "That sounds familiar," the teacher thought. But wait! It's not the world . . . it's . . . no, it can't be! But it was her classroom.

Naturally, I discover that there are some real disadvantages to having a giant classroom, especially since *everything* is giant.

In the writing area Misty and Richie were writing in their writing books. The books were as big as a parking lot. Misty and Richie jumped onto the giant stamp pad and wrote the words by walking back and forth on the page, making letters with inky footprints. "I don't know if we'll be able to publish these. Only Clifford the Big Red Dog could read them," said Richie. "Anyway, who could type on that typewriter?" said Misty. . . .

A model like this is helpful because it allows the children to follow my writing process easily. They know which parts of the story are true because they have participated in the situations I describe. They can see the seams where I have woven truth and fiction together.

Ellen, like many teachers in the early grades, has found that good fiction occurs in all kinds of classroom situations. Teachers like Ellen have used fiction with their students to write their way to new understanding about fiction, writing, and classroom life.

ACTION: EXPERIMENT WITH WRITING SOME FICTION OF YOUR OWN.

Much mystery surrounds the writing of fiction, but you can enjoy writing fiction without writing full short stories or novels. Begin today by purchasing a small, spiral-bound notebook in which you can try some ten-minute writing experiments. The most important thing is to find the most comfortable way to write. It is easier for me to compose on a computer, but some people compose on large sheets, others in small pocket notebooks, and still others on typewriters. All you need is a writing instrument, a surface to write on, and the willingness to set aside ten minutes a day to compose.

Here are a few guidelines for writing short, ten-minute experiments in fiction. Start at the beginning. Write rapidly for ten minutes making few changes to the text and using as much detail as possible. Listen to your words, follow the images, and let the story line run its own course. As an example, I'll choose a memory from my own school days, compose for ten minutes on my computer, and transform my memory into a story that might have happened when I was in sixth grade. The following is the rough first draft:

Mrs. Cottle wasn't smiling. She stood in front of the class, hands folded in front of her. We were usually quite noisy after recess and

Mrs. Cottle didn't mind, she figured that was something natural for children to do when they came inside. Just the way she stood told us we'd better be quiet . . . and quickly. She cleared her throat, "Hmm Hmm," then started slowly and deliberately, "Children, no, I'll use different words, men and women, yes, that's what I'll call you from now on because some serious things are happening to our country and everyone is going to have to do their part."

I liked the idea of growing up, all of a sudden too because my parents were always saying, "Someday . . . someday," with a kind of hopeless tone as if I'd never quite get to where a young man ought to arrive.

Mrs. Cottle went on. "Japan and Germany have declared war against us. Mr. Stetson, the principal, has just told us that our local board is going to need help from every citizen in town and that includes you. We need to save all our papers, at school and at home. Collect steel, aluminum, save electricity. Things are going to be different but I know we will all do our parts."

I raised my hand, "Can we start now, Mrs. Cottle?" If this was war, then I could fight my way; I could help. The rest of the class were colored by the excitement of doing something for their country—now.

This piece of fiction is based on my sixth-grade classroom in East Greenwich, Rhode Island. Those were serious moments during the first—and succeeding—days of the war. I've tried to convey the feeling we had of wanting to do something for our country, along with growing up. My parents despaired that I'd ever get moving fast enough or stop dreaming long enough to grow up. "Some day" were discouraging words to me. If I were to continue with this piece (and I may), I'd tell about a boy learning to grow up during wartime, painting the feelings of patriotism, following the war, and the joy of serving our community. War brought people together in those days in a very different way than it does today.

When I wrote about that occasion, I had to decide where to

begin. For a split second I almost started with "War came to East Greenwich, Rhode Island, with an abrupt announcement." Instead, I decided to show the event through a person, the sixth-grade teacher, although it didn't actually happen that way. Nevertheless, I did see my sixth-grade teacher, Mrs. Fortin, as the person who made the announcement.

I'll try one more experiment to see what happens. I'll try something more fantastic, which for me is much more difficult, something futuristic about schools. Here is the rough, first draft:

Trevor looked forward to school today. He'd actually attend. Monday through Wednesday he had carried out several assignments at the local electronics plant. His voice activated computer had done up six pages of interview material where he'd asked Mr. Blothom about the future of voice activators for children and education. Mr. Blothom seemed pleased with his questions. Today was the day he actually shared the information with the other children who were out on many different assignments. Trevor was pleased with his copy.

The school, in conjunction with Astro Activator Incorporated, had voice activated computers that recorded children's utterances for composing letters, assignments. As fast as a Trevor could talk, the computer, designed to recognize his voice, could print out, on demand, his thoughts and messages.

Trevor didn't actually have to bring in his printouts. Through his home modem he could send messages to friends and send it into his teacher, Mr. Andrade, for a reading and a response. Mr. Andrade read his paper on Tuesday and, using his own voice activator, sent a message back to Trevor telling him some new questions to thnk about asking Mr. Blothom.

But today was his favorite day, the sharing. Trevor and Danny Donahue have video phones their parents had purchased to go with their voice activators. Something parents were encouraged to do to enhance their children's education wherever they could. The video phone, plus the voice activator stuff, made Trevor want to see

Danny more than ever. There was something special about the live event when they could look at each other in the face and tell jokes about their experiences from field experiences. There were also the "read aloud" times in school that were equally special. Children laughing all together in a room gave him a different feeling that laughing onthe video phone which sometimes three or four boys could dial in at once.

Well, I assure you, this was a new experience for me. I have written practically no fiction in my life, much less something "futuristic." Those last ten minutes were pure invention and not very easy either. I have to admit I did get fascinated with voice-activated computers and video phones and what they might mean for schooling in the future. I was obviously discovering as I went along. Then there was the question of how Trevor felt about "in-school" vs. "out-of-school" learning. I liked the feel of his wanting to be with friends face-to-face. Although this was only a ten-minute piece of fiction, like so many others, I'd like to come back to work on it. I wonder what would happen when Trevor went to school. I'd like to interview an expert on the future of technology and dream about how this technology might be written into a story for young children, even speculate on the future of schools for children, because I'd like to know. I suspect they would too. I find that writing fiction gives me a perspective on the present I can't get in any other way.

Such experiments work when you try them every day without missing a day. You will need at least a week to begin to get the feel of working with fiction. Therefore, practice writing one ten-minute fictional piece each day for a week. Whether you write with children, at home, or in school, the key is to write. Here are some ideas for sources of fiction.

• A classroom problem. Write about an occasion that shows a solution (like Ellen Blackburn Karelitz's piece, "The Giant Classroom").

- An event from your own school days. Write a fictional account of the old days.
- An event from your own home.
- Someone on the street, or shopping in a store. Write an episode:
  - as a first-person account, almost as personal narrative.
  - as a bizarre exaggeration.
  - from three different points of view.
- A caricature of a school foible.
- An animal you know. Try writing the piece from the animal's viewpoint.
- An event in history you know well or a current political event. Write about it as if you are actually there.

These are merely suggestions. You will find many other sources for your own use as you become an observer of people and the situations in which they find themselves. Every act between persons is a small piece of an unfolding story, a short piece of fiction because we never know the full story. Take what you see and expand it into a much richer account of a story that "might be." Enjoy.

*see how writers work
with fiction*

One of the intentions of this book (with the Actions that continue) is to notice how other writers write fiction. I've chosen some areas to examine in order to discover how writers for children compose their fiction. We'll look at these elements:

- First lines.
- Leads.
- Introduction of characters.

We'll be looking at how authors handle their writing with a view to our own writing, and we'll also consider how to help children do the same with their own fiction.

FIRST LINES   First lines are very important. From a writer's perspective, the first lines are a window to the entire work, and they can be so for the reader as well. Let's look at what some writers have done with first lines:

It was a dark and stormy night.
                              A Wrinkle in Time, Madeleine L'Engle

Walking back to camp through the swamp, Sam wondered whether to tell his father what he had seen.
                              The Trumpet of the Swan, E. B. White

Henry Huggins was in the third grade.
                              Henry Huggins, Beverly Cleary

Once there were four children whose names were Peter, Susan, Edmund and Lucy, and it has been told in another book called The Lion, the Witch and the Wardrobe *how they had a remarkable adventure.*
                              Prince Caspian, C. S. Lewis

The dim wagon track went no farther on the prairie, and Pa stopped the horses.
                              On the Banks of Plum Creek, Laura Ingalls Wilder

17

Autumn had come too swiftly.
> *The Black Cauldron*, Lloyd Alexander

One sunny morning her mother, Mrs. McColl, woke Katie Morag early.
> *Katie Morag and the Two Grandmothers*, Mairi Hedderwick

Mr. and Mrs. Mallard were looking for a place to live.
> *Make Way for Ducklings*, Robert McCloskey

Many, many years ago in here lived a small boy named Giovanni who had no mother and no father.
> *The Clown of God*, Tomie de Paola

A few observations about these first lines are in order. Several of them are mood setters, like those from *A Wrinkle in Time* and *The Black Cauldron*. E. B. White lets us know that Sam has seen something, yet won't tell his father. As readers, we wonder what he has seen, and the text also prompts us to ask questions: Why won't he tell his father? What kind of man is Sam's dad? C. S. Lewis provides a transition from the first book in his Narnia series to the second, hardly skipping a beat as the four central characters walk from one story into the other. Laura Ingalls Wilder lets us know that her family had just made a long trek and had come to the end of that journey. Mairi Hedderwick introduces her central character, Katie Morag, by informing us that she is a McColl and will have a special day because her mother is getting her up early. Tomie de Paola takes a classic tale and uses a classic opening, "Many, many years ago. . . ." First lines are signals of what is to come. When well chosen, they allow us to construct whole novels by providing a framework.

As John Gardner (1985) points out in his discussion of fiction writing, authors are often unaware of the symbols or structures their language suggests. They do what they do simply because it feels or sounds right. My observations, therefore, ought to be taken with a modicum of caution. You will see more than I do. But speculation and examination are fruitful for our growth as writers and readers.

LEADS

Leads usually refer to the opening paragraphs of a story or book. Leads, like opening lines, set the stage and tone for the entire piece. Note how E. B. White follows his opening line in *The Trumpet of the Swan*:

"I know one thing," he said to himself. "I'm going back to that little pond again tomorrow. And I'd like to go alone. If I tell my father what I saw today, he will want to go with me. I'm not sure that is a very good idea."

White first embeds questions in his text, then answers them through Sam's decision to go back to the pond. Sam is a very definite young boy who makes decisions on his own, even to the point of not including his father. Sam's character is revealed very early in the piece, a characterization that will be consistent throughout the entire book.

Mairi Hedderwick also builds her story quickly through the lead:

One sunny morning her mother, Mrs. McColl, woke Katie Morag early.
"Hurry up, now!" she said, drawing back the curtains. "Here comes the boat. Granma Mainland will be here soon, and you've still got this room to tidy for her."
Granma Mainland lived far away in the big city. She was coming to stay with them for a vacation.
Katie Morag went with her other grandmother, Grannie Island, who lived just across the Bay, to meet the boat.

Although this is a picture book, Hedderwick's words set the stage for the important event, the arrival of Granma Mainland.

ACTION: SPECULATE ON WHAT IS POSSIBLE IN THE REMAINDER OF A STORY BASED ON THE LEAD.

A lead is a like a promise. E. B. White promises that Sam will return to show us what the boy has seen, and quite probably he will go alone. Mairi Hedderwick promises that Katie Morag will meet Granma Mainland during a special day. Have children look at the lead sentences in their own pieces and in the pieces of professional writers to see how these promises are kept and what kinds of stories can be constructed out of first lines and the sentences that follow them. A first line or lead is a development of possibility. Based on these lines, and these lines alone, help children to develop the rest of the story.

It is not uncommon for children who have already read a story to tell what happens later, but they rarely base their telling on what is shown in the lead. "This is what I think will happen because . . ." is the opening to speculation. The "because" means that they will use facts to support their hypothesis about what is to come. As an exercise, mini-lesson, or question used in conference, this kind of speculation can be helpful to children in comparing their own writing with the work of professionals in order to see how good beginnings bring readers in and help them construct what is to come. Writers who set up questions that readers want to have answered create interesting texts. It is the readers' desire for the unfolding information that urges them to read ahead. If children know what kinds of information authors reveal, they will be able to construct more effective texts in their own reading and writing.

CHARACTER
INTRODUCTIONS
Authors bring characters into their pieces in a variety of ways. Here are some examples of how they are *first* introduced:

Sam was eleven. His last name was Beaver. He was strong for his age and had black hair and dark eyes like an Indian. Sam walked like an Indian, too, putting one foot straight in front of the other and making very little noise.

Sam, the main character, is first introduced through two short sentences, as in an oral introduction: "Sam was eleven. His last name was Beaver." This is quickly followed with a glimpse of his face and then a look at how he reveals still more of himself, walking like an Indian.

Notice how Meg, one of the central characters in *A Wrinkle in Time*, is introduced. L'Engle introduces Meg through circumstance—how she behaves in a variety of situations.

The house shook.

Wrapped in her quilt, Meg shook.

She wasn't usually afraid of weather. It's not just the weather, she thought. It's the weather on top of everything else. On top of me. On top of Meg Murray doing everything wrong.

School. School was all wrong. She'd been dropped down to the lowest section in her grade. That morning one of her teachers had said crossly, "Really, Meg, I don't understand how a child with parents as brilliant as yours are supposed to be can be such a poor student. If you don't manage to do a little better, you'll have to stay back next year."

Again, we don't actually see Meg, but we feel with her. What child hasn't known the feeling that everything is going wrong? Poor Meg is not only failing, but her teacher suggests that her parents have only "supposed" intelligence.

Some characters are introduced from the "outside" through description, but it is done very quickly in a few lines:

Mr. Hanson, *On the Banks of Plum Creek*:

His hair was pale yellow, his round face was as red as an Indian's, and his eyes were so pale that they looked like a mistake.

Prince Ellidyr and his horse, *Black Cauldron*:

His hair was tawny, his eyes black and deepset in a pale, arrogant face. Though of excellent quality, his garments had seen much wear, and his cloak was purposely draped to hide his threadbare attire. The cloak itself, Taran saw, had been neatly and painstakingly mended. He sat astride a roan mare, a lean and nervous steed speckled red and yellow, with a long, narrow head, whose expression was as ill-tempered as her master's.

Character descriptions are much like cartooning. Often, authors choose only a few characteristics—hair, teeth, eyes—to represent the entire person. We see people only through the head, in much the same way young children attend to adults. Prince Ellidyr, however, is described fully, along with his horse, suggesting that the two are one.

We have been reading as writers read. We enjoy the story and the unfolding dramas of people as they live in the pages of these books. However brief our experience in writing fiction, we can begin to read the fiction of other writers with a view to how they approach their craft. Now let's move from our own writing and reading to working with the children's own fiction, beginning with actions that help us describe characters in Chapter 4.

4

*experiment along
with children*

My approach to working with children and fiction is one of experimentation. "Let's try this and see what happens," or "Oh look, see what Maurice Sendak has done here. I wonder what it might be like to try that." We take the young author's writing seriously. At the same time, there are useful tools we can show growing writers. Through observing the writing of other authors and understanding the intentions of children, we can help writers to grow in their work with fiction.

ACTION: CHOOSE A CHARACTER NOT YET DESCRIBED AND EXPERIMENT WITH A DESCRIPTION.

The following is a mini-lesson that can be used with children whose stories include characters that readers have not yet "seen." The lesson may succeed with some young children, but I suspect it won't have much broad application before third grade. For the younger years (grades 2–4) you may want to work with a small group. On the other hand, for much older children (grades 5–8) you may find it useful to work with an entire class. Students usually use a separate piece of paper for experimenting with character description. If they like what they have done, they may wish to incorporate their sketch into their piece. In other instances, the description may be apt, yet for the sake of the story it is better to let the character be known through dialogue.

Use an overhead projector where appropriate. Speak aloud about the person you will describe and then demonstrate in a few lines how to "show" that person in the piece. For example, in the two selections I wrote, I didn't actually describe any of the characters. I'll go back and do it here, and I'll try to blend the descriptions with the story itself so that the appearance of the person enhances the story. (The new part, the description, is in roman.)

Mrs. Cottle, in the war story:

Mrs. Cottle wasn't smiling. She stood in front of the class, hands folded in front of her. Her face had a ruddy earnestness about it, and her hair, about which I knew little, seemed more in place this morning than usual. Her eyes, usually relaxed and friendly, had a round, no-nonsense glint to them.

Trevor, in the voice activator story:

Trevor looked forward to school today. He had a hurried look about him. His face seemed to lean forward from the rest of his body as if it wanted to be the first to arrive at school. The rest of his body trailed after him. The back of his head wasn't brushed, and his new, thermal shirt, complete as both shirt and coat and guaranteed for comfort at twenty below, wasn't put together in the back. The cold might wake him up.

I've tried to blend in the description so that it enhances the story. In both instances, I've tried to show how the circumstances affected the person. Mrs. Cottle was serious; Trevor was in a hurry. I suggest that children first write descriptions independent of the story. Let the blending come later, since it is a much more advanced step. Still, some may want to try it.

My directions to myself and to the children during this mini-lesson are the following:

DON: Look back in your folders and find a selection in which you have a favorite character, or one you think is interesting, and describe the person on another sheet of paper. I'll show you what I mean by taking one of my characters and writing about that person on the overhead projector. This doesn't mean that you'll necessarily use what you've written, but I would like you to see how description works in order to show what people are like in your written fiction.

Later, after the children have written their descriptions, several options are appropriate:

1. Examine texts to show how professional writers have blended the description into the story.
2. Have children look over their stories to see where readers might like to see the characters they've described on their separate papers. They may decide they don't fit at all.

PLOT   I've circled plot long enough. It's time to talk about it. Plot is at the heart of fiction. Children seem to sense this, since they immediately focus on action in their writing. Often their problem is that action, the beginning of plot, is everything. This is what John Gardner (1985) says about plot in *The Art of Fiction*:

> *Plotting, then—however childish and elementary it may seem in comparision with the work of surgeons, philosophers, or nuclear physicists—must be the first and foremost concern of the writer. He cannot work out his sequence of events without at least some mention of where the characers are to be or where the action is to take place, and in practice he will never design a plot without some notion of what its elements imply. To say that plot must be the writer's first concern is not to say that it is necessarily the first thing that dawns on him, setting off his project. The writer's first idea for the story—what Henry James calls the "germ"—may not be an event but an interesting character, setting, or theme. But whatever the origin of the story idea, the writer has no story until he has figured out a plot that will efficiently and elegantly express it. Though character is the emotional core of great fiction, and though action with no meaning beyond its own brute existence can have lasting appeal, plot is—or must sooner or later become—the focus of every good writer's plan. (p. 56)*

Children want to begin with plot. But the connection between plot and the rest of the elements that make the plot effective takes a lot of work. These elements require demonstration by the teacher and extensive work with literature, which helps children learn to read as writers and write like discriminating readers. In time, children learn that everything is connected to everything else. As Gardner writes,

Thus plot not only changes but creates character: By our actions we discover what we really believe and, simultaneously, reveal ourselves to others. And setting influences both character and plot: One cannot do in a thunderstorm what one does on a hot day in Jordan. (One's camel slips, or, from homesickness, refuses to budge; so the assassin goes uncaught, the President is shot, the world is again plunged into war.) As in the universe every atom has an effect, however minuscule, on every other atom, so that to pinch the fabric of Time and Space at any point is to shake the whole length and breadth of it, so in fiction every element has an effect on every other, so that to change a character's name from Jane to Cynthia is to make the fictional ground shudder under her feet. (p. 46)

There are so many elements that work together to make good fiction it is difficult to know where to start. One aspect of this book that bothers me is the implication that fiction should be taught or learned systematically: first work on the first sentence, then a lead, then character description, etc. When the child has developed all of these separately, voilà—effective fiction is born. That's the anatomy of the process, perhaps, but how all those ingredients work together is what the art of writing is all about.

ACTION: COMPOSE FICTION TOGETHER AS A CLASS.

I've tried to deal with the many ingredients in writing fiction through a workshop, in which a class composes a story together. I lead the first composing sessions, but I also seek to bring children in to take my place in later sessions. What follows here are excerpts of my session with one class. Note the ways in which I question the class, summarize periodically, challenge, point out inconsistencies, and so on.

DON: I'd like you to come sit here on the floor or in chairs. Above all, it will be important for me to see you so that when you have a contribution to make I won't miss it. So, scrunch in close together. [*We are working in a corner of the room with probably no more than six feet from myself to the person in the back and no more than ten to twelve feet between children on the sides.*]

We are going to create a story together and as we do it, you are going to decide what happens, who the characters are. Things that happen decide the next things that happen. We'll do this so we can get a feel for all the things that go into a piece of fiction, and some of the questions authors ask themselves you can ask each other.

We're going to decide what goes into it, and I'll keep asking you questions to create the story. First, pick one problem to be solved. Try three and we'll talk about each. What could happen?

CHILD: Could have a mystery.

DON: Okay, a mystery. What's the mystery?

CHILD: Someone stole a book.

DON: Let's have a couple more.

CHILD: A murder mystery, people getting killed.

DON: Tell me more. Who killed the person?

CHILD: I don't know.

DON: We have two so far, a mystery with a stolen book and someone killed.

CHILD: There is going to be a kidnapping. Someone is missing, but we don't know if they are killed or not.

DON: So, we have three problems: a missing book, a murder, and someone who is missing. We'll vote on the three. Okay, looks like it is the missing person. [*Note that I continually restate details suggested by the children. Votes are taken on essential elements that go into a story: plot, characters, character names, descriptions of characters, etc.*]

The tone of the session is one of challenge. Note the following interchange:

DON: Tell me about the person who is missing.
CHILD: He is rich and famous.
DON: Why was he rich and famous?
CHILD: He wrote a book.
DON: Tell me about the book.
CHILD: It was a mystery book.
DON: What was special about the book?
CHILD: It was a big seller.
DON: What made it a big seller?
CHILD: It had certain things in the book . . . like jewels.
DON: Did that make it famous? We have a problem now. We have a person who is famous now, rich, has written a book, and we wonder why it became a best-seller.
CHILD: It was an imagination grabber. The book explains what it is. It made people want it most. Your main dream was in the book and people identified with it.

In this beginning segment of the workshop with the children, the pattern of story construction with the leader becomes evident:

- Plot: General.
- Characters:
  - Names.
  - Appearance.
  - Example of typical behavior.
- Setting.
- Specific plot action: Beginning.
- Unfolding plot revealing characters.

Notice that the role of the leader is to call for the specific story components, then to query until children connect them to the main thrust of the story. Here is an example of a review of details following the introduction of a character, and the addition of details about other characters:

DON: All right, let's look at what you have so far: a rich man, Mr. Mint, who is a writer, talkative, tending to brag about himself, who lives in Hollywood and is currently working on a screenplay. His daughter, Claire, is studying to be a nurse in a Boston hospital; she works very hard, is friendly, outgoing but a little stuck on herself because of her wealth. She likes to manipulate people so they will come around to her way of thinking, and you are going to have her kidnapped in the Boston Common after her boyfriend tells her to sit on a bench while he gets her an ice cream cone. Now, tell me about the kidnappers.

CHILD: It is a man and a woman.

DON: Tell me about the man.

CHILD: He has a tattoo.

DON: Why does he have a tattoo?

CHILD: He got it when he was in the service?

DON: You still didn't say why.

CHILD: Well, all the guys on his ship wanted to get one so they had like a bond with everyone having this tattoo.

DON: What did the tattoo look like?

CHILD: It was a ship sailing on the ocean like.

DON: There was some reason you chose a tattoo, called attention to it because it has to have something to do with this story.

CHILD: The kidnapper and Mr. Mint have the same tattoo. See, Mr. Mint was in the service too about twenty years ago, and he was on the same ship with the kidnapper, and the kidnapper never forgave him for something he did to him, and he is going to get back at him by kidnapping his daughter. It's revenge.

CHILDREN: Yeah, revenge.

Again, the basic pattern is to push for details, then challenge the children to integrate the details with all that has come before. The child who related the tattoos to both Mr. Mint and the kidnapper did just that. In the next step in the sequence, we chose names for the kidnappers. Ordinarily, I'd have the children choose the names first, then go into the details of what the kidnappers were like. In this instance, one child started with a tattoo and I pressed the children to take the story from there.

As I look at the transcript, I am struck by the abrupt, hard-driving tone of the interchanges between myself and the children. But I assure you, the children love the challenge of high expectations. What the transcript does not convey is the tone of delight, discovery, and hard work in the workshop.

Although I have outlined a rough sequence here, authors don't necessarily begin with plot. They can begin anywhere. After the children have had several experiences composing stories, I will vary the beginning and have them start with a setting, or one character, or a chance line someone speaks.

ENDINGS

ACTION: STUDY THE LAST LINES IN BOOKS AND HAVE CHILDREN RETHINK SOME OF THEIR OWN LAST LINES.

Writers work hard on last lines and the ends of pieces to leave readers with the impression they intend. After all the work on plot, mood, conflict resolution, and so on, the writer thinks carefully about the last line. Let's examine last lines from the same books we reviewed for first lines in Chapter 2:

But they never learned what it was that Mrs. Whatsit, Mrs. Who, and Mrs. Which had to do, for there was a gust of wind and they were gone.

A Wrinkle in Time, Madeleine L'Engle

As Louis relaxed and prepared for sleep, all his thoughts were of how lucky he was to inhabit such a beautiful earth, how lucky he had been to solve his problems with music, and how pleasant it was to look forward to another night of sleep and another day tomorrow, and the fresh morning, and the light that returns with the day.

The Trumpet of the Swan, E. B. White

"Now that Ribsy is Henry's for keeps, let's think of something we all can play."

Henry Huggins, Beverly Cleary

"Bother!" said Edmund, "I've left my new torch in Narnia."

Prince Caspian, C. S. Lewis

"Look, Caroline," he said, "how Laura's eyes are shining."

On the Banks of Plum Creek, Laura Ingalls Wilder

Taran galloped toward them.

The Black Cauldron, Lloyd Alexander

And Grannie Island never frowned at Granma Mainland's "fancy ways" ever again. I wonder why?

Katie Morag and the Two Grandmothers, Mairi Hedderwick

And when night falls they swim to their little island and go to sleep.

Make Way for Ducklings, Robert McCloskey

The Child was smiling and in His hand He held the golden ball.

The Clown of God, Tomie de Paola

Some endings point to a final mood, a good feeling, as in *On the Banks of Plum Creek*, where Wilder shows Father looking at Laura's eyes. De Paola creates the same mood in *The Clown of God*: the Child smiles with the final step, the golden ball. Cleary resolves the question of Ribsy's future and leaves us with that lovely continuing action, "Let's play." Taran has a story to tell, and Alexander lets us see him ride as fast as he can toward the other riders and home. Taran is entering manhood, and the author lets us complete the story. C. S. Lewis does the same thing with Edmund's flashlight: the children will go back to Narnia; the story isn't over yet. The picture books have a different approach; here, the endings are much more final. McCloskey has the ducks go to sleep on their island. Young children's own fiction often ends with going home or to sleep, and so it is with the ducks. Hedderwick ends the conflict between the two grandmothers with absolutes: "Grannie Island *never* frowned at Granma Mainland's 'fancy ways' *ever again*."

Try a fifteen-minute mini-lesson now. Write a different ending to one of your own stories and have the children take another piece of paper and write a new ending to one of theirs. Or, if some children wish, have them write an ending to a story they have not yet written (this is often more difficult, but some may wish to try it). Various types of endings are possible, as we have seen in the examples. In some, the action ends; in others, the action is continuous, allowing the reader to compose still another story. Particular moods accompany the endings. Some say, "Let's explore"; others say, "Let's just sit here and enjoy the feeling." Some writers, like White, turn us inward as Louis turns to savor the beautiful world around him. Others, like Alexander, turn us outward, to race ahead, to tell the news.

Have children choose a piece and bring it to the mini-lesson. They may decide not to use what they write in the mini-lesson at all, but they will learn from participating in the exercise. Some children may need to discuss their options before they start to write. Sometimes when I work with children I write an ending to a piece of my own fiction. I could even write one now for each of the pieces I wrote in my two fiction experiments in Chapter 2. I'll write for five minutes on each:

Every one of us, dressed in our Sunday best, scrubbed until we hurt, followed Mrs. Cottle to the reviewing stand to receive our awards.

Trevor looked at Mr. Andrade. For just a moment in the meeting of eyes, he knew they'd be able to have another day at school that week.

The second is more continuous, suggesting a resolution to the story—that the children will have more time at school, and that Trevor and Mr. Andrade will have what they want in this extra schooling. It is a turning point rather than an ending. The first example, however, is more final. The class, with Mrs. Cottle, wins the award after much hard work.

These are only a few of the different kinds of mini-lessons you can try with your children. When you write fiction with them, you will discover other types of mini-lessons that will be helpful. Not all children will be writing fiction at the same time. Some will write poetry, some will pursue nonfiction, while others will record personal experience. Share your own writing and your experiences with mini-lessons with your colleagues.

respond to children's fiction

Whether children are reading or writing fiction, my response is basically the same, because in both cases, the children are composing a text, either one they start themselves (writing) or one that has been started by another author (reading).

When I approach a child who is reading or writing fiction, I first want to know how the work is going, and only then get into what the piece is about:

TEACHER: How's it going?
CHILD: Okay. No problems.
TEACHER: What's it about? Just tell me quickly without telling me the story.
CHILD: It's about a boy who has lost his horse, and he's trying to think like a horse to find him.

Children should get used to stating the essential agent and action in a work, whether it is one they have composed themselves or one they are reading. The child's quick summary of a piece is the best place on which to build a writing conference. Even if the child is stuck and replies, "It's going terribly. I don't like it. It's boring," I'm still interested in the one- or two-sentence statement that tells what the piece is about. Now the child may say, "Oh, I don't know what it's about; that's the problem, it could be X, or Y, or Z." This is a good example of self-diagnosis and an even better foundation for a conference than the case of a child who simply says, "I don't know what it is about." Actually, the child who sees options and recognizes possibilities, even if stymied by them, is ahead of the child who has drawn a blank.

When I worked with Leslie Funkhouser in her second-grade classroom and the children had been reading trade books for the first forty-five minutes of the morning, we used to pull them over on the rug for a quick check of where they were and of their perceptions of what their books were about. They would sit in a circle cradling their books in their laps. We'd go rapidly around the circle in order, with the children holding the covers

37

of their books so all could see them. We'd tell them, "Say quickly what your book is about." As might be expected, second graders who had more difficulty abstracting would try to tell the entire story thus far. "No, no," we'd say, "just say it quickly; we don't have time now for the entire story." This directive made them select the essential agent and action; a class of twenty-five would take four to five minutes—maximum. This technique was also a quick and effective way to keep tabs on what children were reading and on their understanding of book essence. Children were also able to keep in touch with what the other children were reading, recognizing books they had already read that were being read by their friends. This same approach could be used with the children's own writing. Or, in classrooms where reading and writing are carried on simultaneously, children can share their own reading or writing by giving the title and author, and the essential agent and action.

My main focus in the conference on fiction is plausibility and flow. Do the children know where they are headed, and is their sense of direction based on a plausible understanding of events in the piece? Even if I haven't read the child's writing or the book the child has nearly finished, I can still ask the questions that quickly construct the child's understanding of what has and will transpire. I move quickly from main idea to characters because these should determine the direction of the piece. Here are some samples:

TEACHER: You say your piece is about the good guys killing the bad guys. Who are the good guys? What are their names?

CHILD: Uh, I don't know. They are just good guys; that's all.

TEACHER: Where are they from? When does this take place?

CHILD: Uh, they're um . . . uh . . . from another planet and this is in the future.

TEACHER: What would be a kind of name you could use for

that? Names are so important for readers, yet they can be hard . . . like for the future. Want to think about it?

Names, as we shall see in the data about children's fiction in Chapter 6, are very important. The building of characters is connected with thinking through names. Soon, with enough focus on the names in both trade books and the children's own writing, it becomes more automatic for children to ask each other for help with names. I might even supply a copy of dictionary pages listing all kinds of names. (Many dictionaries include such lists.) Of course, children can make up names or coin new ones that are suggestive of the kind of character they are creating. When reading a trade book, I'll often ask the child if the names chosen by the author sound appropriate.

My next line of questioning after the name is established is to determine what type of person the character is and what makes him that way. Even if the name still keeps things generic for character development, I'll push for more specifics, then go on from there:

TEACHER: You call these men "men of the future." Do they have a leader? Tell me about the leader.

CHILD [*usually composing on the spot*]: Oh wow, uh, Rakor. How does that sound?

TEACHER: Sounds of the future, and now tell me about him. You said he is a good guy? What has he done that is good?

CHILD: Oh, he is smart. He is the smartest one of the whole bunch.

TEACHER: What did he do that is smart? With his men or how?

This kind of pushing may seem tedious to both you and the child, but it is vitally important to work on it, because so much of the violence in children's "good guy–bad guy" writing results from the lack of a sense of person or motive—a reason for shooting or fighting. Somehow, space weapons diminish the need for true-to-life characters. The child in the arcade merely pushes a button and zap: the plane and person disappear. No blood, no person, gone, out of sight, but dead nevertheless. On to the next killing.

Little in Saturday morning television, children's Christmas toys, or video games encourages any connectiveness between violence and character dimension. Characters do not ponder options or reflect on the consequences of their actions. Children can maintain categories: Oh, that's fiction; this is real. Our task, even though fiction is "unreal," is to make it good fiction and to approach the multiple dimensions of life that ought to be included in it. The children will be used to this type of questioning. When a child is reading a book, I often ask about characters in the same way as in a writing conference:

TEACHER: Oh, you are reading *Henry Huggins*. What's it about?

CHILD: It's about this kid who lived in a town and he was bored until this dog came along.

TEACHER: What's Henry like?

CHILD: Well, I just got started, but so far I know he likes dogs and has always wanted one. He is persistent because he really works on his mom for the dog. He can also give a good name to a dog. The dog is thin and so he calls him "Ribsy."

TEACHER: Yes, I get the feel of what Henry is like from those details. What do you think will happen next?

CHILD: I think he will play a lot with the dog and they will have adventures together.

Conferences about children's work in reading and writing involve all the ingredients we've looked at in the chapter so far. The conference serves more as a way to learn about what strikes a child than to develop a question-and-answer session. I ask questions with the "of course you have considered these matters" tone. We discuss leads, dialogue, endings, plot, language, character description—everything that should be part of a piece of fiction, whether the child has read it or written it.

ACTION: CONDUCT SMALL GROUP CONFERENCES ON CHILDREN'S FICTION.

The small group conference is geared to discussing books and writing. Conferences can focus on particular authors—i.e., a group might consist of children who have read several Beverly Cleary or Maurice Sendak books, or the Narnia series.

There will be children who are reading and writing fiction at the same time. Call them together as a conference group to examine the nature of fiction, both through their own writing and through the writing of the professionals whose work they are reading. The conference is intended more for general discussion of the writer in relation to the subject than to help children make their pieces sound like the work of authors they read. Children may want to experiment with dialogue, character description, or leads as an offshoot of what they are reading. Teachers may sense that it is right to encourage a particular child to experiment in her own writing with a feature modeled from a professional.

ACTION: HELP CHILDREN TO PLAN THEIR FICTION.

Fiction writers have a notion of where their pieces are going before they start. Of course, some characters develop in ways the author couldn't have anticipated, and the entire process of a book has to be changed or the plan abandoned. Still, unless there is some prior notion of where a piece is going there is no logical base from which to depart. Authors usually know when they are moving away from a plan; they are aware that the path their main character was going to take has now assumed an entirely new twist.

Planning writing—or anything—is not necessarily a natural

act for young children. Children's early writing more closely resembles play, particularly the fiction that enters the world of pretend, even if it only uses drawings and words. I watch young Michael draw his guns and planes, and the sound effects that escape his lips are the same as those he uses when he pushes a bulldozer across the floor to dump dirt in his dump truck. He has only a general plan, if any, of where his play will take him. He doesn't look back while moving from action to action; his final act, destroying the truck, has little to do with his first intention to use it to build a road. He transforms events to suit his fancy. As the author, he is the truck driver, general contractor, and the pilot who decides to drop a bomb on the truck, ending play. Action is the central focus, and he represents all the characters. When young children play together in the early years, their play is largely in parallel, that is, they play next to each other, exchanging progress reports and play-by-play descriptions of what is happening, but their play does not interact.

Helping children learn to plan begins by helping them to know where they have been in order to sense the logical direction of their work. They need to have a sense of the concrete before they can move on to an abstract representation of what is to come. A child has a large 12-by-18-inch piece of paper with a large space at the top for drawing a picture. I know she will write after she has drawn the picture; this is her characteristic pattern. She knows she will write as well. Yet if I ask her what she will write after she draws—before she has even drawn the picture—she will usually come up with a blank. She may say, as children often do, "Wait and see," or "I haven't drawn the picture yet." In short, the easiest planning for this child will be to decide what she will write next, after she draws the picture or writes the first sentence. She needs external cues as a base from which to plan, because she does not know in her head beforehand what the entire piece will include.

The following list profiles children's development as planners and indicates appropriate places for teachers to extend a child's current practice toward more advanced approaches to planning:

1. *No plan, just a general statement.* This is going to be about trucks.
2. *The child draws and reports on other ingredients that may also go into the picture.* There is no action yet, no narrative, just the dumping of ingredients that go with this type of picture.
3. *The child draws and tells a story about the ingredients.* The child constructs a story orally, although a story is not represented in the picture. The child may also represent some of the ingredients in words. In a more advanced representation of this development, the child may write and name the elements:

   This is a boy. This is a truck. This is a house. This is a pool.

   The latter child can also tell the teacher what he may write next, since he can consult the drawing.
4. *The child draws with logically connected action in the drawing.* The action is usually episodic. There is an agent causing the action, and there is an object of the action. That object or person may react to the first action (e.g., a gun is drawn, the gun fires at a plane; the plane fires back; end of episode), and there may be four to a dozen such episodes in one drawing. The general title of this type of drawing is "War," or "The Good Guys and the Bad Guys."
5. *Narrative text—drawing after writing.* When the child is able to compose a connected narrative without drawing for rehearsal, he can usually cite a plan for the text in advance of writing. This will include a main action or a problem with a beginning, middle, and end. The child has enough background in writing, drawing, and explaining to others about what he has done in the past that he is

now able to represent the past well enough to project into the future, to state what will be. Once a child has an idea of what a piece will be about, he can talk about it and even get into the process he might use to construct it.

At this point, planning fiction with a child before a piece is underway is fruitful. The planning might go like this:

TEACHER: Tell me about your piece.

CHILD: I'd like it to be about this dog who is always in trouble.

TEACHER: Does the dog have a name?

CHILD: I think the name Rascal would fit.

The discussion can then follow the same rough pattern of composing fiction used in the class demonstration on pages 29–32. The difference, however, is that this discussion is quite brief and involves only key action, agent (possibly bringing in the dog's master if he has one), and several incidents. With this, the child is off and writing. Bear in mind that just because the child has a plan doesn't mean he is able to hold to it. At first, the teacher may have to make notes and leave them with the child to aid remembering.

6. *First plans.* When a child is able to articulate what she wishes to include in her fictional piece, a written map representing what will come can now be more useful to her. Because she has written fiction and has a strong story sense, she can deal with the abstraction of a map, web, or scheme. Figure 5–1 is an example of a plan—or brainstorming—that might follow from my piece on my sixth-grade experience (pages 11–12). The first items on the map are Mrs. Cottle, myself, and the principal, Mr. Stetson. I know there will be a contest to see who can collect the most for the war effort. That sort of goes in the middle column. Then I wonder about the prize. I figure a presentation by Bob Feller, the famous Cleveland Indians

FIGURE 5–1   PLANNING, OR BRAINSTORMING

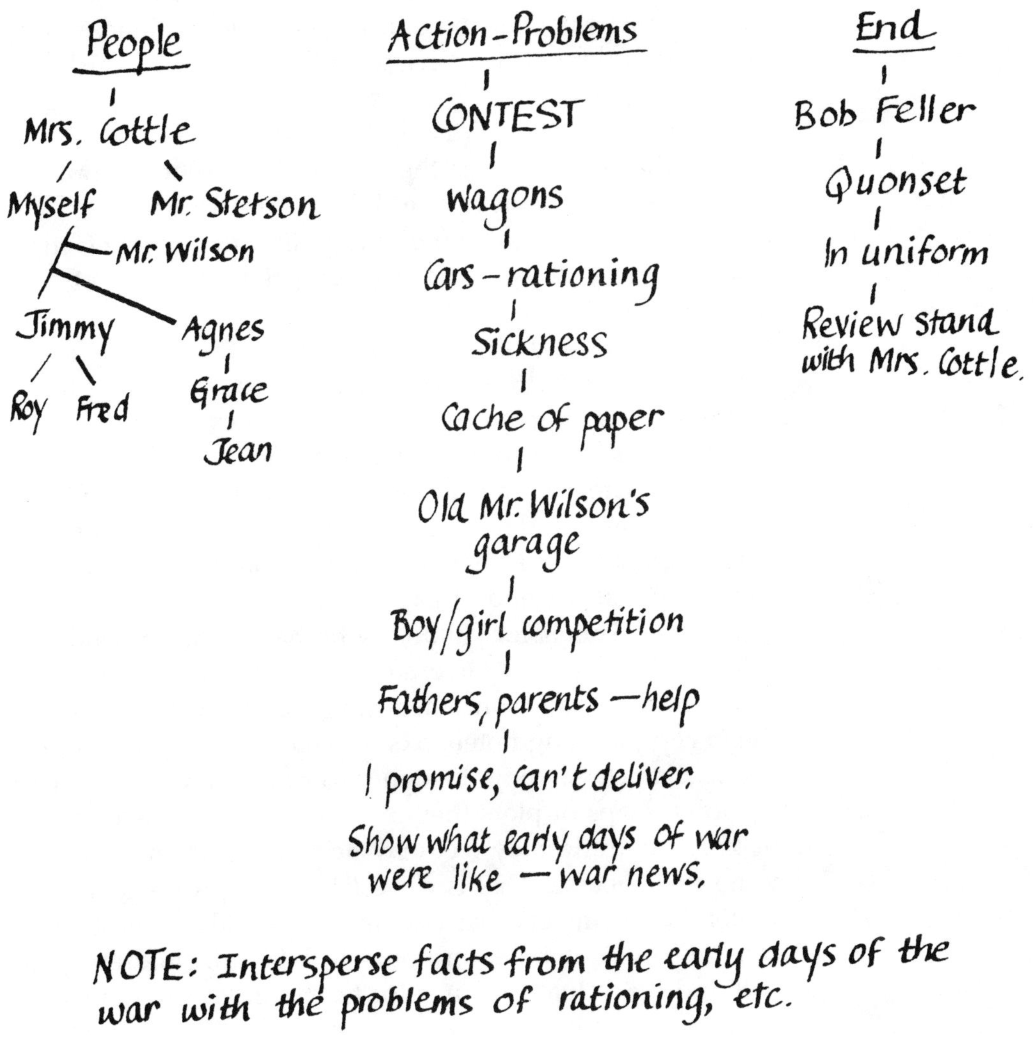

People

Mrs. Cottle

Myself   Mr. Stetson

Mr. Wilson

Jimmy   Agnes

Roy   Fred   Grace

Jean

Action–Problems

CONTEST

Wagons

Cars – rationing

Sickness

Cache of paper

Old Mr. Wilson's garage

Boy/girl competition

Fathers, parents — help

I promise, can't deliver.

Show what early days of war were like — war news.

End

Bob Feller

Quonset

In uniform

Review stand with Mrs. Cottle.

NOTE: Intersperse facts from the early days of the war with the problems of rationing, etc.

baseball player who is nearby at Quonset Point, in full uniform, would be quite an incentive. That goes down third. So there is a beginning, the agents, then the outcome. Now for the plot problems, the obstacles that stand in the way. This becomes a growing list: illness, a need for little red wagons to collect with, boy/girl competition, help from parents—on the last day getting help from kindly Mr. Wilson, who has a garage full of papers that put us over the top. I also needed more characters for the boys vs. girls part, and I put down these names. Finally, a note to myself: "Intersperse facts from the early days of the war with the problems of rationing, etc."

Some children get launched so far into their pieces it is very difficult to help them. They are already wedded to impossible and implausible plots when they yell for help on page twelve. In this instance, I recommend that some children see me or have a planning conference before they start (a definite understanding that I have worked out with each child). I may ask a few others to have conferences at the end of page one.

7. *A final step.* This is for children who have written fiction extensively and who have already demonstrated the ability to map and plan when they write. Suggest that they keep planning notebooks in which they record notes about characters, copy dialogue from their favorite books, jot down maps of plots they may like to use some day, or keep anything they feel may help them when they write their fiction. This is closest to what professional writers do. I suggest that you, as teacher, also keep that same type of notebook for yourself. Like the children, you will find it a valuable source for teaching, writing, and learning.

Caution: Although I have labeled this the most advanced step of all and have implied that children who have demonstrated the ability to abstract through maps, etc., are not yet ready for the planning book, I still trust children's judgment. If a child thinks she has it within herself to pursue this approach, I'd ask her how she intends to go about it. If the child has a strong enough impression of what to do, then I'd let her run with it. I have a hunch that the child will go to the nearest store to buy a notebook anyway—with or without our approval.

ACTION: READ FICTION ALOUD TO THE CHILDREN.

When teachers read fiction aloud, it allows children to try on different writers' voices by listening to the stories as the teacher reads. Listening is as much a composing act as reading a text is; one comes from words read aloud, the other from print on the page.

Reading aloud to children is a very necessary part of any literacy program. It is neither a luxury nor an afterthought. It is the place where children sense what it is to be an audience, entertain various possible outcomes together, and experience the joy and power of the written word. A strong story with a precise storyline makes children want to try the craft for themselves, as well as read the authors they have shared together through reading aloud.

FINAL REFLECTION The wish to tell stories, to explain the world of wonder and terror around us, is an essential part of being human. Children enjoy writing fiction, in order to play, but also to explore a world filled with action. By representing that action in drawing and writing, they can be a part of it.

For many people, life seems staid and boring in comparison with the adventures portrayed on television or in the works of professional fiction writers. But as long as we see only the action, without the physical or human agents behind it, life will be boring indeed. The beauty of the art of writing is that it can bring together the person and the act—the person suspended between one situation and what is nearly possible or what is nearly possible just around the corner, which leads the story on, unfolding the author's promise. It is the fulfillment of such promises that makes the writing of fiction such a challenge. In a way, it is the most difficult of all the genres to teach and therefore requires hard work on the part of the teacher. That hard work begins with our own exploration of fiction through reading and writing.

Because children's first fiction so closely resembles play, children are unaware of the demands of the genre. In addition, children today live in the age of television, which provides little depth in its characterization of people and their lives. Television is an action medium where agents demonstrate little motive or reason for what they do. To counter this influence teachers must show children how fiction can teach them about what they want to learn and become. By composing stories with the children, reading stories aloud to them, and examining the writing of professionals to see how they work with leads, endings, plots, and character, teachers can open the door to a multidimensional world rich in detail, incident, and meanings.

a new look at children's fiction

Much of children's early fiction is reminiscent of their play. Through their drawings and words they reconstruct powerful forces or live the lives they wish to lead. In the same way, children read fiction in order to become the very characters they read about. What writing offers them is the opportunity to control the action themselves, to construct the play situation most pleasing to them.

Like their play, children's early plots are centered in action: "The good guys beat the bad guys." Highly egocentric in structure, their stories offer us no names, descriptions, or motives for the characters, who simply act. If a child wants to make a piece more exciting, he simply adds more action; with young boys the action is frequently violent, with little plausibility for the violence. Way back in 1972, in my first work on children's writing, I found that early male fiction was characterized by action-reaction couplets, the "He hit 'em, he hits 'em back" kind of writing. Evil people do bad things; good people get revenge. A second look, however, shows that the focus (and fascination) is on the cataclysmic events, not the agents themselves—the explosion, the trajectory and blast of the rocket, or the ingestion of the duckbill by Tyrannosaurus rex.

Children learn to write fiction just as they learn to draw: they begin with a caricature of what fiction is. When children first draw, their drawings are noun dominated. An object (sun, flower, or mother) simply exists on the page. When two objects appear, there is the possibility of action or object relationship on the page, and that is often the beginning of narrative. Up to this point, the child may merely have written "bt" (boat) underneath the drawing of a boat. With the addition of a sun, however, the child moves on to a sentence of naming: "The bt is slg" (The boat is sailing). But these drawings show no action or motion marks, and characters are stiff and not drawn in profile; they stare out at the viewer.

By the time children choose to write fiction, they are very much centered in action—the doing—especially boys. Nouns are the pawns of verbs. Action controls. View how the writing actually goes down on the page: each episode triggers the next episode, and there is little rereading or reexamining of the text for location. A triggers B, B triggers C, etc. If there is to be character development or a plausible motive, the child will need to read and reread in order to link agent with action.

I invite you to take a trip with me to look at children's fiction at the Stratham Memorial School in Stratham, New Hampshire. The data I will share here is a small part of a larger study led by my colleague, Professor Jane Hansen, of how children, teachers, and administrators, and researcher's values about reading and writing, change over three years. At the same time, I invite you to examine the fiction in your children's writing folders. I'll share some theories about the meaning of what I see, and you'll do the same. Sometimes you'll agree with me and sometimes you won't. You'll see exceptions in what your children do, and you'll say, "I've got a different theory." Then you'll change how you work with fiction.

WHERE TO BEGIN I'll begin with a look at how children create characters in their stories. I didn't arrive at this choice quickly. I took a look at what professional writers have said about the importance of character development in Donald Murray's collection of writers speaking about writing (1987). Here is what some of them have said:

Joyce Cary:

I begin, that is, not with an idea for a book, but with a character and a situation. Then, if both seem to be useful and significant, I write a few pages to show that character in that situation. Sometimes this description of a character and a situation grows into a book.

Vincent McHugh:

From first to last, the novelist is concerned with character. In the novel, everything is character, just as everything is tone or process. Each event must be focused in a human consciousness. Without someone to look at it, there is no landscape; no idea without someone to conceive it, and no passion without persons.

John Irving:

The voice I love best is the narrative voice, is the storyteller's voice. I believe that narrative momentum must override description, must restrain all our pretty abilities with the language. . . . The only thing (in my opinion) that narrative momentum must not override is character—for the building and development of characters, even narrative must pause and waits its turn.

"Wait a minute," you are saying, "what do these writers have to do with my first-grade children?" Well, writing is writing and fiction is fiction. Regardless of age, fiction places certain demands on the writer for the sake of the reader. In short, actions are determined by people. Because of particular human natures, events occur. But this isn't where children begin.

WHERE CHILDREN BEGIN   Children's first fiction writing is like a cartoon. It is cartoonlike because they choose only the essential, stereotypical elements of fiction to put into their stories. They want the story to be "exciting, humorous, interesting." Their plots are often exaggerated. Here is a text by Julie Fawcett, a first-grade child:

This is the princess and the bad guy is trying to kill the princess. The princess has been thrown off the wall of the castle. The princess is being rescued from Mister Prince. The princess has been rescued by Mister Prince. They want to get married. They are going to date a while before we get married. They are looking at a house.

The child has composed a story in which a problem is addressed: a princess is in the hands of an evil one. Rescue results in love, dating, marriage, and ultimately a house. A complete story.

The characters exist, however, for the author's own ends: she wants to live out their actions. The characters are not developed. We don't know why the bad guy wants to kill the princess or why the princess and the prince want to get married. Their motives are assumed. The child feels no need to make them explicit. I suspect she is living through the princess, and that is enough. Note the line "They are going to date a while before *we* get married." The child writes for herself; she invests the piece with her own self-interest.

SHARED CHARACTERS Through the first three grades, most of the characters that appear in children's fiction are already known by the other children in the class. In short, the characters were not invented. I have put the types of "shared" characters in children's fiction into three classifications:

1. Generic and popular.
2. Friends.
3. Self/first person.

Examples of generic and popular figures are good guys, bad guys, monsters, sharks, princes and princesses, Snoopy, Garfield, Little Bear, Santa Claus, Transformers, doctors, and commanders. I call them generic because there are certain formulae that go with each character. The minute a child uses the word Garfield, he has already chosen a conventional plot to go with the character. The other children are familiar with Garfield, who needs no description, since most already know what he looks like and his characteristic personality traits, and therefore have certain expectations of what will go into the story.

Good guys and bad guys seem far less specific, but Saturday

morning television (which has a great influence on children's early fiction) has even defined those two types of characters. One of the first-grade teachers at Stratham School was trying to get a child to assign a name to the "good guys." "You know, you have a name like Joshua. Don't the good guys have a name too?" The child just blinked, not understanding the teacher, and the name "good guys" stood. Later, Brenda Miller, then a doctoral student who had done an extensive investigation of first-grade writing genres, informed the puzzled teacher that these "good guys" and "bad guys" had already been manufactured as plastic figures in the children's TV marketplace. In fact, their given names were "Good Guys" and "Bad Guys."

Children also use their friends—another shared name—in their early fiction: in trips to outer space, sleepovers, fishing and hunting trips, and early mysteries. Once again, the names are already known by all the children. Teachers often hear children say, "When are you going to put me into one of your stories? I wrote about you yesterday in mine." Or, "You are almost going to get killed in this story, but you'll be okay."

The first person is also used in writing fiction. This is a shared name because the children in the class already know the author. The use of first person does not rule out the simultaneous use of friends or even generic character types.

Writing is a highly social act. Children want to be seen as authors. In our first study of reading and writing (Graves and Hansen 1983), we noticed a significant phenomenon: children felt that an important moment had come when one of them wrote fiction. They felt that a child who wrote fiction, even with shared names, had crossed an important line into authorship. Thus, in rooms where children publish and regularly share their writing, classmates have much to do with how fiction is approached. Quite possibly, this may contribute to a need for shared characters that is greater than that in classrooms where there is less sharing. For those of you who teach in grades one and two, check your children's writing folders to see if there is any character invention and the proportion of shared characters in the children's writing.

CHARACTER
INVENTION AND
INTRODUCTION

When children invent characters, there is much to explain to a class that regularly shares their writing. Questions quickly arise: "Where'd he come from? What does he look like? Who is he?"

Inventions of characters in this particular study of early writing were more on the humorous side. It was almost as if the children were saying, "I'm going to play, have fun, and create something new and funny." For example, in the following piece, Erin McAlexander introduces a new name and character, a Wackaduce.

One day Me and Amy went walking in the park. Then I saw a Wackaduce. It looked gross and I mean gross. Amy had a seizure when she looked at it. It's eyeballs came out and it smoked a pipe. His hands come off and his head comes off. He lives in a chalk board. Then, he looked hungry.

This third-grade author feels the need to explain her invention to the class. She cites an extra authority, Amy, who "had a seizure when she looked at it." Even though the author has drawn the Wackaduce in a picture, what differentiates this piece of character introduction is that she actually describes the outside of the new creature in words as well as shows it in a drawing.

Sometimes new characters are introduced through dialogue. Another third-grade author, Deveny Schroeder, mixes plot, dialogue, and character introduction in the lead to her piece:

MARDY AND ALVIN MEET

One day a boy ant was at the park with his sister and his dad. The boy's mother had died in a car accident long ago. The boy was swinging on a swing. Then a caterpillar said, "Hi, do you want to play with me?" "What is your name?" asked the caterpillar.

> *"My name is Alvin," said the ant in a bored voice.*
> *"Hi Alvin."*
> *"Oh ya, this is my sister Victoria," said Alvin who was jumping rope nearby.*
> *"Hi," she said, "I'm Victoria."*
> *"Hi," said the caterpillar.*
> *"By the way," said Alvin, "What is your name?"*
> *"My name is Mardy" said the caterpillar.*
> *"That's a nice name" said Alvin.*

Several features stand out in this introduction. Characters are introduced in much the same way that children work together: "Hi, what's your name?" The sound or quality of a name is also mentioned: "That's a nice name." I can almost hear the author congratulating herself on her ability to create names.

Jeff Rohr, a fifth-grade author, uses the first-person characteristic of the detective fiction genre to introduce characters in the opening paragraph of his mystery, "Secret Passage":

> *I was in Kentucky visiting my grandfather's farm. I was with my best friend Chuck and oh, of course, my eight year old brother, Tim. Chuck and I both were 12. Chuck was kind of short. He had blond hair and blue eyes. He was a little chubby not fat just kind of rugged. I myself was a medium size tall about five feet. I have dirty blond hair and brown eyes. Tim has brown hair and some freckles. He was the size of any eight year old. His two front teeth were missing and every time he grinned he looked like Count Dracula.*

Sizes and ages are important to Jeff, and his descriptions deal with the above-the-neck details of teeth, hair, and eyes. Jeff is like many children, who, beginning in about the fourth grade, enjoy creating characters that are two to five years older than their current ages. Many ten- and eleven-year-olds in this study created characters who dated, drove cars, went to junior or senior high school, and suffered the usual adolescent embarrassments.

Fifth-grade author Dan Dolan, along with several companions, read many of Lloyd Alexander's books. Entranced by Alexander's new lands and characters, they sought to create new settings and adventures of their own. Following the example of their favorite author, the boys tried a different kind of character introduction, revealing their characters through action, as in this introduction to Danny's piece, "The Land of Merewhere."

THE LAND OF MEREWHERE

It was dark and the only sound was the soft bleating of the sheep in their pens. All was quiet, too quiet. The night watchman scanned the yard outside the fort from the tower. The slight whisper of an arrow leaving its bow was heard in his ears. The arrow hit its mark and the watchman fell with hardly a dull thud to the ground, an arrow protruding from his chest.

Dawn came with the clatter of dishes in the mess hall. Dangward, the old warrior, had his meal of oates and barley and with a satisfied belch left his seat. He was about to walk in the door to his cottage when he saw something out of the corner of his eye. It was the body of the watchman. He ran over to him and hanked the arrow out of his stomach and asked him if he was alright.

The watchman, deeply wounded, answered with a no. Dangward ran to get Mirco, the Doctor. Mirco came and looked at him.

"It doesn't look good," he said. "It looks as though he is going to die."

"But Mirco," said Dangward, "You have to save him he is the only man with a trade in all of Merewhere beside the smith and potter!"

"The wound is deep," said Mirco. "You do not know how to remove an arrow, Dangward."

"Then it is my fault he will die," said Dangward through clenched teeth, "I will find who did this to him."

Notice how Dangward is revealed in the way he crudely gets up from the table and then bullishly removes the arrow from the chest of the night watchman. We don't actually get an exterior description of any of the characters, yet they are revealed in subtle actions and in interaction with each other. Dan's story went on for another thirty-three pages, the plot moving plausibly according to the personalities of the characters.

I find that when children begin to get into significant character development, they choose one character to carry the story. In Dan's story it is Dangward. Other characters soon emerge with more specific personalities than this writer has demonstrated in the past, but their development is dependent on the strong main character. For example, Mirco is revealed through Dangward's blunder with the arrow. We find Mirco to be a forthright physician as he upbraids Dangward.

Dan balances many skills in his creation of "Merewhere," so many that you wonder, as I did at first, "What did the teacher do to help a child write such a piece?" Although his teacher, Mary Ann Wessels, conducted the usual conferences and offered encouragement, there was no way she could directly affect Dan's sense of story, plot, character, and language. On the other hand, she did provide a challenging classroom where children discussed their writing. I suspect that her most important contribution was to allow Dan to read everything Lloyd Alexander has written and to spend a month on the writing of "Merewhere." In short, it is indirect teaching such as Mary Ann's that has a far greater impact on children's artistic expression than the "direct" teaching of skills.

Much more research needs to be done to study the influence on a child's own writing of reading one author extensively. When children read an author as a writer, they more naturally integrate an overall sense of balance, language selection, and the relationship of part to whole needed to keep a piece moving into their own composing frame. Some children learn best by concentrating on reading one author and composing one story over a long period of time. Such reading can't be forced; yet when a child pursues that one author to learn the author's composing secrets, a new kind of learning takes place that is seldom seen in school curricula.

ACTION: REVIEW YOUR CHILDREN'S READING PATTERNS.

Ask the children to look into their records of trade books. Tradebook records can be similar to those used for writing. The outside of the reading folder carries a brief accounting of books read, with the title, the author, and the date the book was started, ended, or abandoned (See Figure 6–1). The inside of the folder carries letters children may have written to each other or the teacher about the books, reviews, or journal entries. A few children may periodically like to rate the books in descending order of their preference, or may want to list all the books read by a particular author on one page. As a final step, you may find it useful for your children to identify their favorite character in the work of a given author. Are there any similarities between that character and the characters in their own reading and writing? Which children are interested in even examining the similarities or conducting these exercises?

CHARACTERS IN THE PROCESS OF GROWING UP

Children often explore the years just ahead of them through adolescent predicaments and dialogue. Melissa Keefe, a ten-year-old author, writes about fifteen-year-old Pam, who is called to the portable phone while she is swimming in the pool behind her home:

"Who's calling?"
"This is Linda."
"She is in the pool right now."
"Just a minute!" yelled Pam as she flipped off the board. She climbed out of the water, her flowered bathing suit that said "CALIFORNIA" across it was sopping.

FIGURE 6–1　READING FOLDER RECORD

Date Started	Title	Author	Date Completed or Abandoned
Sept. 7	*The First Four Years*	Wilder	Sept. 13
Sept. 14	*On the Banks of Plum Creek*	Wilder	Sept. 26
Sept. 27	*Ramona the Pest*	Cleary	Oct. 2
Oct. 2	*Prince Caspian*	Lewis	Abandoned Oct. 4
Oct. 4	*Felita*	Mohr	

> "Hello?"
> "Hi Pam?"
> "Yeah,"
> "This is Linda."
> "Linda who?"
> "Linda Wadashka."
> "Do I know you?"
> "Yes, I'm in your social studies class."
> "Oh, you are the girl who always gets A's right?"
> "Yeah, I guess. Well, anyway I'm having a pool party a week from tomorrow. Would you like to come?"
> "Oh gee, I have plans."
> "Oh, alright then, Bye."
> "Bye Linda." Quickly Pam pickedup the receiver and dialed her best friend's number.
> "Hello, is Karen there?"
> "Yes."
> "Within this lifetime Scott." Pam said to Karen's little brother."
> "GET OFF THE PHONE!" screamed Karen.
> "NO!" Scott screamed back.
> "YES YOU NERD!!" Smack! Scott ran off crying.
> "Hello?"
> "Hello Karen, this is Pam."
> "Oh hi!"
> "Speaking of nerds you know who just called me?"
> "Who?"
> "Linda Wodashka!"

The easy, duplicitous conversation with Linda and the fight to get the phone from a "nerdy" little brother who gets linked with another "nerd" are everyday events in the life of any fifteen-year-old. Melissa's piece is filled with telephone conversations and a sophisticated handling of other adolescent personalities. Later, Melissa introduces a new character, Kayla, at a sleepover. Sixteen-year-old Kayla is the central figure in the story, and Melissa describes her with a well-practiced eye for detail:

Kayla put her bags on the bed. She was wearing stone washed jeans, a yellow turtleneck with a white sweatshirt that had ten buttons. She also was wearing tree torns. Her hair was pulled back in a banana dip to show off her dangling earrings. She had blue eye shadow, very light pink lipstick and a little blush. Her hair was blond accenting her blue eyes.

Quite possibly Melissa has been influenced by the series of young romance books, *Sweet Valley High*. Nevertheless, like many young people in the upper-elementary years, she "tries on" the older years through fiction and the use of dialogue. I shared this observation with Nancie Atwell; she believes that this experimentation with dialogue and clothing closely resembles girls' play with Barbie dolls and the dialogue that extends from the types of characters developed in play.

Embarrassment is a familiar theme in the writing of children approaching adolescence. Again, the characters are revealed principally through conversation. Lisa Rowe, a sixth-grade student in our study at Stratham Memorial School, demonstrates this in the lead to her piece, "The Big Wedding Embarrassment":

"Don't make me walk down the aisle with an 8 year old creep," said the age 11 girl.
"Do it for your cousin Vicki," Mrs. Cantaloupe demanded.
"But Mom!"
"Angelica if you don't Vicki and Dave will be very upset with you."
"Ok, but do I have to go arm and arm with him?"
"Yes," said the lady I call Mom.
"Such humiliation," I murmured.

Lisa demonstrates a rich sense of character in the dialogue between Angelica and her mother. We don't actually see the characters, but we certainly hear realistic dialogue, from her mother's appeal to altruism to Angelica's protests and the final *sotto voce* statement, "Such humiliation."

The process of growing up, especially in adolescence, involves the rehearsal of thousands of conversations that are never revealed: "And he'll say, and I'll say, and then I'll say again." Whether these are love duets or arguments with friends, parents, or siblings, they are part of elaborate preparations for adulthood. Young people find that their contacts with others are often erratic, with high risk of personal embarrassment and possible loss of friendship. Growing up is a risky business, and since so much of growing up involves negotiations with others, children practice endless conversations within their heads, in play, and through their own writing. I find that Melissa's elaborate external descriptions of her characters are the exception. Most of the time, dialogue is the more usual source of character revelation for children in the upper grades.

ACTION: REVIEW SAMPLES OF CHILDREN'S DIALOGUE.

Children like to write dialogue. This is true from the beginning. They enjoy the life that comes from their character creations. Dialogue gives breath and humanity to the person. Try the following review exercises with your children:

1. Find some dialogue in your writing folders. Find a place where people are speaking. Find a place where, if you were to read that part aloud, you'd hear the actual words of the person.
2. Find a place where more than one person is speaking, where the people go back and forth in conversation.
3. You may find several places where you have lots of dialogue. If so, find the one you think shows best what the people in your story are like.

You have probably noticed that I have involved the children in each of the actions in this chapter. The very process of examining folders is helpful to the child in most cases. The children become partners in research. From time to time, the children themselves may come up with ideas for folder review that might interest the entire class. The more they participate in the process of review, the more you will have up-to-date information about children's fiction and the teaching of reading and writing. Why should you do all the work? What you find out by yourself without the children's involvement is one further step toward excluding the people who the need the information most—the children.

You may wish to collect the data the children gather about their use of dialogue. If you do, here are some further steps you might want to follow in examining the dialogues. Although some of these steps may be advanced, there are some children in your classroom who may be able to do some of them. In order to sense the children's preparedness for examining their work, conduct a mini-lesson using some of the pieces of fiction you have written yourself:

- Is there turn-taking in the dialogue?
- Do the characters react to each other or speak alone?
- Are there distinctive elements of personality in the dialogue?
- Is a character identifiable by the speech he/she/it uses?
- Does the dialogue connect with the plot or does it exist as an excuse to have talking?
- Does the writer use language to qualify the dialogue? (For example, ". . . he said angrily.") Was the qualifier necessary?
- Is the dialogue blended into the narrative?

These questions are merely entrees into looking at how your children use conversation in their writing. Beware of hierarchical thinking. Art exists to break rules. These questions are designed most of all to help you see what your children are doing. They are a way of trying to understand children's intentions in their composing. Any tool that helps us understand children's intentions also shows us how to understand the proximal zone of their current composing. The challenge in teaching is to understand and extend children's intentions.

REVIEW TO THIS POINT

How children develop and use characters is an important index of how they are growing in their ability to write fiction. The creation of a human being is a highly sophisticated act, whether in sketching, acting, sculpting with clay, or using any other creative medium. Children's first drawings show crude stick figures, because the child selects body parts to suggest "personness." Most assuredly there will be a head, with some elements in the head to indicate eyes and mouth, followed by a torso and sticks for arms and legs. No question, there is a person there, but the full details of personness are missing. Even more sophisticated, however, is the person in context, in interaction with the surrounding world, or the precision of the moment when the person is revealed to universal understanding. I think of Michaelangelo's portrayal of the creation of humankind in the Sistine chapel: God extends a finger, and man reaches toward it, palm upturned to receive life. The power of the entire event is captured in the *gap* between the finger and the palm.

Yet how natural for children to represent human beings. They want to understand life by creating the most important creatures in their lives, people and animals. When they begin, they discover creation by playing at it, and playing means selecting caricatures of the event much as a cartoonist will abstract the essence of a person in a few quick lines.

Children begin with what they know. In our study, children started with their friends and generic creatures like monsters, sharks, and princesses. They used action stereotypical of the creature they created: monsters and sharks eat, destroy, and "get you," and princesses are in danger and eventually get married. In one sense, children cartoon their own early uses of fiction.

Motion, action, something happening that won't be boring: these are great concerns to children. Not unlike the overuse of exclamation marks and interjections in early writing, the high-action event, particularly the violence and high body counts in boys' writing, seems to take charge. People exist for the carnage; the action does not result from plausible, unfolding events.

The creation of a named character introduces the class to someone they don't know and thus seems to place greater demands on the writer. In one sense, the child is creating the genre of a person, *that person*, and must therefore supply such elements as dialogue, external description, and more plausible connectedness and consistency of action. This doesn't always happen, of course, and the class starts to ask questions in order to understand the new character: "Did you draw him?" "Let me see him." "What did he do that for?" "How did you think him up?"

Notice in Figure 6–2, a summary of how characters are used by children at the various grade levels in Stratham, that there is a particular time span for certain character types. For example, generic types run from first grade through fourth grade. The use of friends in pieces of fiction extends from first grade through sixth grade. In this limited study, the use of friends trails off in grades four and five, then picks up again in sixth grade as children include each other in adventure stories. The use of dialogue begins slowly and continues to increase through the sixth grade. Children start to help us see their characters through words in grade three, and this continues to increase through grade six. (Since children represent their characters through drawings in grades one and two, in one sense they see less need to use words to describe their creations.) Finally, through first-person stories and through created persons, children begin to reflect on the events around them. Amy Mason, a Stratham sixth grader, wrote a piece involving a time warp in which a child goes into a closet. While she is there, time stays "present tense" for her while her family ages many years.

FIGURE 6–2   CHILDREN'S USE AND REVELATION OF CHARACTERS IN THEIR FICTION

Grade	Generic	Friends	First Person	Created Names	Dialogue	External Description	Internal Reflection
1	▬▬	▬▬	▬				
2	▬▬▬	▬▬▬	▬▬▬	▬	▬▬		
3	▬▬	▬▬▬	▬	▬▬	▬▬	▬	
4	▬	▬▬	▬▬	▬▬▬	▬▬▬	▬▬	
5		▬▬	▬▬	▬▬▬	▬▬▬	▬▬▬	▬▬▬
6		▬▬▬	▬▬▬	▬▬▬	▬▬▬	▬▬	▬▬

▬▬   Minimal use
▬▬▬   Moderate use
▬▬▬▬   Extensive use

Amy's piece could be called internal reflection, since it is told through her eyes, with family members looking back at her death while she was in the closet:

". . . got into Harvard College this year. I'm very proud of him. Lori was very smart too. Too . . . (sniff) she passed away."
I'm dead? I quickly got back to the conversation.
". . . she was never found. She died on her 13th birthday. She was last seen when she was in her closet. Johnny locked her in her closet as a joke and we all went downstairs. After ten minutes we heard banging on the door, so we rushed upstairs but it was too late. She stopped banging. Her Father tried and tried to get her out. There was a big clothes hanger that jammed the door, but when we got the door open, she was gone.
"And she was such a nice girl," my uncle said.

Later, Amy reflected on the event through Lori:

"I'm going to find out why I'm dead," I said to myself. And I went downstairs to the living room. "I wonder what year I'm in," I said while picking up the remote.
"Well, at least they still have the same garbage on T.V." I said. "Oh, oh, someone's coming."

ACTION: SURVEY YOUR CHILDREN'S USES OF CHARACTERS.
You may wish to use the chart on page 68 as a way of charting how your children are using characters in their pieces. Try examining three or four children's writing folders to see the type of characters they use and the ways in which they involve them in their stories. Take two boys and two girls as a starter. Using different colored pens for each, just put "Xs" to indicate where their use of characters falls. Obviously, you won't be using the grade levels as categories, only the columns.

The writing of fiction is the telling of a story. Storylines are important. A sense of character and plot is an essential element. For all of our work in charting the use of characters, a strong, plausible story must be dominant in fiction writing. I have chosen to examine character here because the involvement of a strong character seems to produce the most plausible plots, which seem to result in the best stories. There will be obvious exceptions to this.

There must be an element of play in composing fiction or working in any other genre. Along with this notion of play in composing must be the parallel process of "playing" with our teaching. We experiment, toy with, and explore new notions of representing the world in our teaching, as we do in our reading and writing. When we play, we are free to engage in the formulation of theory: "Ah, I think I see a pattern here. I'll ask the children to help me with this one," or "I think I know why she did that. I'll ask her." When teachers "play," when they listen to children in the midst of gathering data in a structured classroom, the class more closely resembles a disciplined writing studio, in which both teacher and children are fearless in their explorations.

references

Alexander, Lloyd. 1965. *The Black Cauldron*. New York: Dell.

Cary, Joyce. 1950. "The Way a Novel Gets Written." *Harper's Magazine*, pp. 87–93. February.

Cleary, Beverly. 1950. *Henry Huggins*. New York: William Morrow and Company.

De Paola, Tomie. 1978. *The Clown of God*. New York: Harcourt Brace Jovanovich.

Gardner, John. 1985. *The Art of Fiction: Notes on Craft for Young Writers*. New York: Vintage Books.

Graves, Donald, and Jane Hansen. 1983. "The Author's Chair." *Language Arts* 60 (2): 176–83.

Hansen, Jane; Thomas Newkirk; and Donald Graves, eds. 1985. *Breaking Ground: Teachers Relate Reading and Writing in the Elementary School*. Portsmouth, NH: Heinemann.

Hedderwick, Mairi. 1985. *Katie Morag and the Two Grandmothers*. Boston: Little, Brown.

Irving, John. 1985. In *Voice Lost—Eight Contemporary Writers on Style*, edited by A. Weir and D. Hendrie, Jr. Lincoln, NE: University of Nebraska Press.

L'Engle, Madeleine. 1970. *A Wrinkle in Time*. New York: Farrar, Straus & Giroux.

Lewis, C. S. 1969. *Prince Caspian*. New York: Macmillan.

McCloskey, Robert. 1969. *Make Way for Ducklings*. New York: Viking.

McHugh, Vincent. 1950. *Primer of the Novel*. New York: Random House.

Murray, Donald M. 1987. Syllabus—Course in Fiction. Durham, NH: University of New Hampshire.

White, E. B. 1970. *The Trumpet of the Swan*. New York: Harper and Row.

Wilder, Laura Ingalls. 1953. *On the Banks of Plum Creek*. New York: Harper and Row.

index